The Tiger and the Monk: Courage and Respect in Zen

Learn Acceptance, Inner Peace and Gratitude with Zen Stories

Kensho Satori

Author: Kensho Satori

First Edition: July 2024

Graphic Design: OpenArt

Typesetting: Carta & Inchiostro

Cover: Hana Design

All rights reserved.
No part of this book may be reproduced,
stored in a retrieval system, or
transmitted in any form or by any means,
electronic, mechanical, photocopying,
recording, or otherwise, without the
written permission of the publisher.

Dedication

To all those who seek inner peace and wisdom in the small daily things.

This book is dedicated to those who walk with a light step, observe with an open heart, and believe, like me, that every moment is a precious gift.

With gratitude and hope,

Kensho Satori

Table of contents

Introduction

What is Zen? Zen is a school of Buddhist thought and practice that emphasizes meditation and mindfulness of the present moment. Originating in China as Chán, the tradition spread to Japan where it became known as Zen. Founded by the legendary monk Bodhidharma in the 6th century, Zen combines elements of Indian Buddhism with Chinese Taoist traditions. Its primary goal is to awaken the true nature of the individual through meditative practice and awareness.

Why is Zen Wisdom Important? In a modern world characterized by fast-paced living and constant distractions, finding inner peace can seem like an arduous task. Zen wisdom offers valuable tools to achieve lasting tranquility and a profound awareness of oneself and the surrounding world. This book is a practical guide combining inspirational stories and fundamental Zen principles designed to help you cultivate a more serene and meaningful life.

The practice of Zen and mindfulness is not a passing trend but an ancient discipline that has helped countless people live more present and aware lives. According to Jon Kabat-Zinn, creator of the Mindfulness-Based Stress Reduction (MBSR) program, "Mindfulness is awareness that emerges through paying attention on purpose, in the present moment, and nonjudgmentally." This simple yet powerful practice is at the heart of Zen philosophy and can radically transform our approach to daily life.

Benefits of Zen Wisdom

- **Inner Peace:** Learning to meditate and practice mindfulness helps reduce anxiety and stress, promoting a sense of tranquility that permeates all areas of your life.

- **Present Moment Awareness:** Mindfulness helps you live in the here and now, improving your concentration and reducing the tendency to worry about the future or dwell on the past.
- **Improved Relationships:** Practicing compassion and gratitude, which are fundamental in Zen, allows you to build deeper and more meaningful relationships with others.
- **Resilience and Adaptability:** Zen stories and principles teach you how to adapt to life's changes with flexibility and acceptance without losing your center.

A Guide for Your Personal Growth This book is structured to offer you a journey of personal growth through Zen wisdom. In the first part, Zen stories of animals will provide powerful metaphors and teachings that you can apply directly to your daily life. In the second part, we will explore the fundamental principles of Zen and mindfulness, offering practical techniques to integrate these lessons into your routine. The third part introduces advanced stories and principles, while the fourth part guides you in exploring and adopting Zen principles for a more serene and fulfilling life.

If you feel that your life is often overwhelmed by stress, worries, and lack of balance, this book is the resource you've been looking for. It offers not only a deep understanding of Zen philosophy but also practical tools to transform your way of living. Through reading and practice, you will discover how Zen wisdom can address your deepest needs and help you overcome your weaknesses, cultivating lasting inner peace and profound awareness.

Begin your journey towards a more mindful and serene life today. Let Zen wisdom illuminate your path, offering you the keys to live a fuller and more satisfying life.

Part 1: Zen Stories of Wisdom and Growth

Tenzin and the Master: The Discovery of Presence

Tenzin was a young monk eager to learn the ways of the Zen master. He had heard of the profound peace and clarity that come from living fully in the present moment and sought to experience it personally. One morning, he approached the master with an urgent question: "Master, how can I live in the present moment?"

The master, with a serene smile, replied, "Tenzin, come with me." They walked to a nearby garden, where the master instructed Tenzin to sit and simply observe his surroundings.

At first, Tenzin's mind wandered, filled with thoughts of the past and worries about the future. He struggled to focus on the present moment. Noticing Tenzin's distraction, the master gently placed a flower in his hand and said, "Focus on this flower. Observe its colors, texture, and fragrance."

As Tenzin directed his attention to the flower, he began to notice details he had never seen before. The vibrant hues, delicate petals, and subtle scent drew him into the present moment. His mind started to calm, and a sense of tranquility enveloped him.

The master then spoke, "Tenzin, the present moment is always with us, but we often ignore it, trapped in the web of our thoughts and anxieties. By bringing your awareness here and now, you discover profound peace and clarity."

Tenzin realized that living in the present moment did not mean emptying his mind but fully engaging with what was in front of him. It meant being aware of his surroundings, sensations, and feelings without judgment.

The lesson Tenzin learned that day was the essence of mindfulness: the ability to be fully present, aware of where we are and what we are doing, and not overly reactive or overwhelmed by what is happening around us. This practice, simple as it may seem, has the power to transform our life experience.

Mindfulness helps reduce stress, improve performance, and gain insight and awareness through observing our mind. It allows us to connect better with others, lower stress levels, and concentrate more effectively. By practicing mindfulness, we cultivate a state of being that brings peace and clarity, enabling us to live more fully and joyfully in the present moment.

Tenzin's journey to discovering presence underscores the importance of mindfulness in our daily lives. It teaches us that by focusing on the present, we can find calm amidst chaos and clarity in confusion. Through mindfulness, we learn to embrace the now, making every moment a step towards greater peace and understanding.

The Journey of the Lonely Elephant

In a distant forest lived a lonely elephant named Kavi. He felt an emptiness inside and a burning desire to discover more about his existence. He decided to embark on a journey of self-discovery and personal growth, leaving his home to explore the world and find answers to his inner questions.

During his journey, Kavi met various animals who taught him important lessons. One day, he encountered an old wise tortoise who said, "Kavi, the key to your personal growth is knowing yourself. Listen to your heart and be open to the experiences that life offers you."

Following the tortoise's advice, Kavi began to pay attention to his thoughts, emotions, and sensations. He discovered that many of his fears and insecurities were rooted in past experiences. He learned to recognize these feelings without judgment, allowing himself to let them go.

Throughout the journey, Kavi crossed rivers and mountains, facing challenges that made him stronger and more aware. One day, while meditating by a stream, he realized that true discovery was not in the places he visited but in the inner journey he was undertaking. He understood that personal growth is a continuous process of learning and adapting.

He also met a group of elephants who welcomed him warmly and helped him understand the importance of connection with others. Thanks to them, Kavi learned the value of community and sharing experiences.

At the end of his journey, Kavi returned to the forest with a new self-awareness and profound inner peace. He had discovered that personal growth is an endless journey of exploration, reflection, and openness to change.

Kavi's story teaches us that self-discovery requires courage and a willingness to explore our inner depths. It is a journey that leads to greater awareness and the ability to live a more authentic and fulfilling life. Every step of the way contributes to our evolution and brings us closer to a deeper understanding of who we truly are.

The Clever Monkey and the Gold Plated Watering Can

In the jungle, lived a monkey named Ramu, known for his intelligence and ingenuity. One day, Ramu found a shimmering gold-plated watering can. Eager to make the most of this discovery, he decided to use it to improve the lives of the other jungle animals.

Ramu began collecting water from the river with the gold-plated watering can and irrigating the plants during the dry season. The plants started to bloom, providing food and shade to the animals. The other animals, impressed by Ramu's ingenuity, thanked him for his wisdom and effort.

One day, however, the watering can disappeared. The animals grew worried, fearing that without the gold-plated watering can, the plants would wither. But Ramu, remaining calm, said, "Wisdom does not reside in the object but in how we use it. We can find other solutions."

Ramu guided the animals in constructing a simple yet effective irrigation system using bamboo and banana leaves. With the new system, water was distributed evenly to the plants, which continued to thrive.

This experience taught the animals that ingenuity and wisdom do not depend on the tools we possess but on our ability to adapt and find creative solutions to problems. Ramu demonstrated that innovation and collaboration could overcome any difficulty.

The story of Ramu and the gold-plated watering can reminds us that true wisdom lies in the intelligent use of the resources at our disposal and in the ability to find practical and innovative solutions. Ingenuity and wisdom go hand in hand, enabling us to face challenges with creativity and determination.

We learn from Ramu that the most precious resource is our mind and how we use it to improve our lives and those of others. This story encourages us to think outside the box and use our ingenuity to overcome difficulties and create a better future for everyone.

The Lotus Flower and the Mist

In the stillness of a hidden pond among the mountains, grew a beautiful lotus flower. Every day, the lotus woke up enveloped in a thick mist, isolating it from the outside world. The mist represented the difficulties and challenges every living being must face, but the lotus, with patience and adaptability, continued to grow and bloom.

The lotus understood that to thrive, it had to adapt to changing conditions. Every morning, the mist slowly lifted, revealing the lotus's beauty. This process taught the lotus the importance of patience. Instead of fighting against the mist, the lotus allowed itself to be embraced, accepting its temporary role in its growth.

The patience of the lotus was a lesson for all living beings. It understood that difficulties are not permanent and that with time, all challenges dissipate like the mist. The lotus did not try to hasten the process but waited calmly, knowing that beauty and strength arise from resilience and adaptability.

One day, a wise monk observed the lotus and reflected on these lessons. He realized that, like the lotus, humans must face the mist of difficulties with patience and adaptability. Only through acceptance and the ability to adapt can we grow and flourish in our lives.

The monk taught others that true beauty lies in the acceptance of the present and adaptation to change. Patience is not merely passive waiting but an active form of trust in the process of life. Like the lotus, we must learn to live in harmony with our circumstances, knowing that every challenge prepares us for a new phase of growth.

This story of the lotus flower and the mist reminds us that patience and adaptability are fundamental virtues. Through acceptance and flexibility, we can find beauty in difficulties and discover our inner strength. The lotus teaches us to see every challenge as an opportunity to grow and bloom, just as it does every morning when the mist dissolves.

The Dancing Monk and the Rainbow

In a monastery perched among the mountains, lived a monk known for his joy and serenity. Every day, the monk danced in the courtyard of the monastery, inspiring anyone who saw him with his harmony and inner peace. One day, after a rainstorm, a magnificent rainbow appeared in the sky. Without hesitation, the monk began to dance under the rainbow, finding in it a deep connection with change and the beauty of life.

The monk taught that life is like a continuous dance under the rainbow of change. Just as the rainbow appears and disappears, so too are our experiences and challenges temporary. The monk emphasized that harmony is found in accepting and embracing change rather than resisting it.

Once, a young novice asked the monk how he managed to maintain his serenity despite difficulties. The monk replied, "The key is to find joy in change. Every shift in our lives is an opportunity to grow and learn. Like the rainbow, challenges and happy moments come and go. The dance of life is about harmonizing with these changes rather than trying to control them."

The story of the dancing monk and the rainbow teaches us the importance of embracing change with grace and joy. His dance was not just an expression of happiness but a symbol of the ability to adapt and find harmony amid change. The monk showed that by accepting and flowing with life's circumstances, we can discover profound inner peace.

In a world of constant change, the monk reminds us that true harmony lies in accepting change. His dance under the rainbow represents the joy of living in tune with life's flow, embracing each moment as an opportunity to grow and find beauty in transformations.

Part 2: Principles of Zen and Mindfulness

Zen and Mindfulness - How Awareness Can Transform Our Daily Lives

Mindfulness, or the practice of being present and fully engaged in the moment, is a cornerstone of Zen philosophy. By paying attention to our thoughts, feelings, and surroundings without judgment, we can experience life more vividly and reduce stress.

Mindfulness helps us break free from the autopilot mode in which we often live. When we are mindful, we are more aware of our actions and their impact, leading to more intentional and meaningful living. By focusing on the present moment, we can improve our concentration and mental clarity, making us more effective in our daily tasks.

Practical Techniques for Mindfulness

1. **Breathing Exercises**: Focus on your breath, observing each inhale and exhale. This simple practice can anchor you in the present and calm your mind.
2. **Mindful Eating**: Pay attention to the taste, texture, and aroma of your food. Eating mindfully can enhance your enjoyment of meals and improve digestion.
3. **Body Scan Meditation**: Mentally scan your body from head to toe, noticing any tension or discomfort. This practice helps you become more aware of your physical state and promotes relaxation.

Mindfulness transforms our daily experiences by helping us appreciate the present and cultivate a deeper sense of gratitude and peace.

Zen and Positive Thinking -

The Power of Positive Thought and How to Apply It

Positive thinking is a fundamental aspect of Zen philosophy, encouraging us to cultivate a hopeful and optimistic mindset. By focusing on positive thoughts and attitudes, we can transform our perception of life and improve our overall well-being.

Positive thinking does not mean ignoring the negative aspects of life but rather approaching them with a constructive attitude. It involves recognizing challenges as opportunities for growth and maintaining hope and resilience in the face of difficulties.

Techniques for Positive Thinking

1. **Affirmations**: Use positive statements to reinforce a positive mindset. For example, repeat phrases like "I am capable and strong" to boost confidence.
2. **Gratitude Journaling**: Write down things you are grateful for each day. This practice can shift your focus from what is lacking to what is abundant in your life.
3. **Visualization**: Imagine positive outcomes for your goals and dreams. Visualization can enhance motivation and increase the likelihood of achieving your aspirations.

By embracing positive thinking, we can create a more fulfilling and joyful life, filled with hope and possibility.

Zen and Inner Peace -

Finding Inner Peace through Meditation and Reflection

Inner peace is the foundation of a balanced and harmonious life. Zen teaches that inner peace can be achieved through regular meditation and self-reflection. These practices help us quiet the mind, reduce stress, and connect with our true selves.

Meditation Practices for Inner Peace

1. **Seated Meditation (Zazen)**: Sit in a comfortable position, focus on your breath, and let go of distracting thoughts. This traditional Zen practice helps cultivate deep inner stillness.
2. **Walking Meditation (Kinhin)**: Walk slowly and mindfully, paying attention to each step and breath. Walking meditation integrates mindfulness into physical movement, promoting a sense of calm and presence.

3. **Reflective Journaling**: Spend time writing about your thoughts and feelings. Reflection helps you process emotions and gain insights into your inner world.

Through meditation and reflection, we can develop a profound sense of inner peace that sustains us through life's ups and downs.

Zen and Compassion - Cultivating Compassion for Yourself and Others

Compassion is a key principle of Zen, emphasizing empathy and kindness towards oneself and others. Practicing compassion helps us build deeper connections and foster a sense of community.

Ways to Cultivate Compassion

1. **Self-Compassion**: Treat yourself with the same kindness and understanding you would offer a friend. Acknowledge your flaws and mistakes without harsh judgment.
2. **Loving-Kindness Meditation (Metta)**: Meditate on sending love and goodwill to yourself and others. Repeat phrases like "May you be happy, may you be healthy, may you be at peace" while visualizing different people.
3. **Acts of Kindness**: Perform small acts of kindness daily, such as helping a neighbor or offering a kind word. These actions can create a ripple effect of compassion in your community.

Cultivating compassion enriches our lives by fostering empathy and strengthening our relationships with others.

Zen and Simplicity - The Art of Living a Simple and Fulfilling Life

Simplicity is a core tenet of Zen, encouraging us to eliminate the unnecessary and focus on what truly matters. Living simply helps us reduce stress, increase clarity, and find contentment in everyday life.

Principles of Simplicity

1. **Decluttering**: Remove physical and mental clutter from your life. Keep only what is essential and meaningful.
2. **Mindful Consumption**: Be intentional about what you consume, whether it is food, media, or material goods. Choose quality over quantity.

3. **Presence**: Focus on the present moment and appreciate the simple pleasures of life, such as a walk in nature or a meal with loved ones.

Embracing simplicity allows us to live more intentionally and find joy in the here and now. By simplifying our lives, we create space for what truly matters and cultivate a deeper sense of fulfillment.

Part 3: Advanced Stories and Principles

The Buffalo and the Yoke: A Lesson in Acceptance -

Acceptance and Adaptation to Life's Circumstances

In the tranquil Japanese countryside, lived an old buffalo who spent his days working in the fields with his yoke. One day, a young Zen monk approached the buffalo, observing him with curiosity. He noticed how the buffalo seemed serene despite the hard work.

The monk, seeking wisdom, asked the buffalo: "How do you stay so calm while bearing such a heavy burden?"

The buffalo, calmly replied: "It wasn't always this way. At first, I struggled against the yoke, trying to free myself. But the more I fought, the harder the work became. Eventually, I realized that accepting the yoke and adapting to my situation would bring me more peace."

The young monk reflected on these words, understanding that resistance to life's circumstances brings only suffering. Acceptance, on the other hand, can transform a difficult situation into an opportunity for growth.

The buffalo continued: "Accepting the yoke doesn't mean giving up. It means recognizing the reality of the present moment and adapting. This allows me to work more efficiently and peacefully."

The monk learned that acceptance is a profound form of wisdom. It involves recognizing life's circumstances without judgment or resistance and finding ways to adapt harmoniously. This lesson taught him to live with greater inner peace, regardless of the challenges life presented.

The buffalo's story reminds us that true strength lies in acceptance and adaptability. When we stop fighting against inevitable situations and learn to adapt, we discover a new form of resilience and serenity.

Accepting circumstances doesn't mean surrendering but finding ways to thrive despite difficulties. Through acceptance and adaptability, we can face life with a calmer mind and an open heart, transforming challenges into opportunities for personal growth.

The Voice of Silence: The Discovery of Inner Peace -

The Power of Inner Silence

In the depths of a peaceful forest, a monk lived in a small temple near a gently flowing river. Every evening, the monk would light a lantern and place it by the river, watching the light reflect on the water. This habit helped him meditate and find inner peace.

One day, a young disciple approached the monk and asked: "Master, why do you light the lantern and place it by the river every evening?"

The monk replied: "The lantern represents our inner illumination. Just as the lantern's light illuminates the river, our awareness can illuminate our mind and heart, allowing us to see with clarity and serenity."

The disciple, curious, asked: "How can we light our inner lantern?"

The monk smiled and said: "The key is the practice of mindfulness. Observing our thoughts without judgment, being present in the moment, and cultivating gratitude for what we have. Just as I light the lantern every evening, we must continually nourish our awareness."

Lessons of Inner Illumination

1. **Mindfulness Practice**: Dedicate time each day to meditation and present moment awareness. This helps maintain a clear and serene mind.

2. **Non-Judgmental Observation**:
   Learn to observe your thoughts and
   emotions without judging them.
   This allows you to accept them and
   let them go, finding inner peace.
3. **Cultivating Gratitude**: Practice
   daily gratitude to illuminate your
   heart. Gratitude helps us see the
   beauty in small things and feel
   connected to the world.

The story of the lantern and the river
teaches us that our inner illumination
depends on our ability to be aware and
present. Through mindfulness, non-
judgmental observation, and gratitude,
we can find lasting inner peace and
illuminate our lives with clarity and
serenity. This constant practice guides us
towards a deeper understanding of
ourselves and the world around us.

The Tiger and the Monk: A Story of Courage and Respect - 118

Lessons of Courage and Respect

In a remote monastery among the mountains, lived a monk known for his courage and wisdom. One day, while meditating at the edge of the forest, he saw a tiger approaching. The other monks, terrified, fled, but the monk remained still, observing the tiger calmly.

When the tiger came close, the monk lowered his gaze in respect and said: "I do not fear you, great tiger, because I understand your wild spirit. We are both beings seeking to live according to our nature." The tiger, instead of attacking, stopped and watched him attentively. It seemed to recognize the monk's courage, and after a moment of silence, it walked away peacefully.

The monks, who had witnessed the scene from a distance, were amazed by their companion's courage. They asked how he found the strength to face the tiger without fear. The monk replied: "True courage is not the absence of fear but the ability to act with respect and calm despite fear. I showed respect to the tiger, and it responded with the same respect."

This story teaches two fundamental lessons: courage and respect. The monk's courage was not just physical but also moral, based on understanding and accepting the tiger's nature. The mutual respect between the monk and the tiger demonstrates that every being deserves dignity and consideration.

Lessons of Courage

1. **Facing Fears**: Courage does not mean being without fear but facing your fears with dignity and determination.
2. **Acting Calmly**: In dangerous situations, remaining calm can lead to positive and unexpected results.

Lessons of Respect

1. **Recognizing Others**: Every being has its nature and deserves respect. Recognizing and respecting others can transform a potential conflict into a moment of mutual understanding.
2. **Mutual Respect**: Showing respect to others, regardless of circumstances, often leads to being respected in return.

The story of the tiger and the monk teaches us that courage and respect are closely linked. Facing life's challenges with courage and respect for others can lead to a more harmonious and meaningful life.

The Golden Carp and the Stream of Life -

Discovering the Flow of Life and Our Connection with It

In a tranquil mountain stream, lived a golden carp who spent her days swimming against the current, exploring every corner of her habitat. Each day, she observed the water flowing incessantly, carrying leaves, twigs, and reflections of light. The golden carp, fascinated by this continuous flow, began to reflect on its meaning and her connection with the water.

One day, while swimming, she encountered an old monk meditating on the riverbank. The carp approached out of curiosity, and the monk, noticing her presence, said: "Little carp, what do you seek in the flow of the stream?"

The carp replied: "I seek to understand the flow of life and my connection with it. I see the water flowing ceaselessly, adapting to every obstacle, and I wonder if I can learn to live like it."

The monk smiled and replied: "The flow of the stream represents the flow of life itself. Just as the water adapts and continues to flow, so must we learn to adapt to life's circumstances. Our existence is interconnected with everything around us. Understanding and accepting this flow brings harmony to our lives."

The golden carp realized that swimming against the current was not just about strength but also about adaptability and understanding the natural flow of things. She learned to follow the water's flow, adapting to obstacles and finding peace in the continuous movement.

Lessons from the Flow of Life

1. **Adaptability**: Like water, we must learn to adapt to life's situations. This does not mean giving up but finding ways to flow through difficulties.
2. **Connection**: Recognizing our connection with the world helps us live in harmony. Every action has an impact, and every event is part of a larger flow.
3. **Acceptance**: Accepting the flow of life means embracing challenges and opportunities with openness and resilience.

The story of the golden carp and the stream reminds us that, like water, we can find strength and serenity in flowing with life, accepting and adapting to its infinite variations. This understanding allows us to live in harmony with ourselves and the world, discovering lasting inner peace.

The Jade Buddha and the Secret of Contentment -

The Secret Art of Contentment and Gratitude

In an ancient temple hidden among the hills, stood a jade Buddha statue. Its serene expression and tranquil smile attracted numerous monks and pilgrims, who sought to discover the secret of its inner peace and contentment. One day, a young monk approached the statue and asked his master: "How can we find contentment and gratitude in our daily lives?"

The master, with a smile, replied: "The jade Buddha teaches us that true contentment does not depend on external circumstances but on our ability to be grateful for what we have and to live in the present moment. Follow me."

The master led the young monk to a tranquil garden and asked him to sit and observe the surroundings. "Close your eyes and breathe deeply. Think of three things you are grateful for at this moment," said the master.

The young monk followed the instructions, and slowly, he began to feel a sense of peace and fulfillment. Opening his eyes, the master continued: "Gratitude is a daily practice. It is not about what we possess but about how we see and appreciate what we have. Contentment arises from acceptance and gratitude for every small gift of life."

Lessons of Contentment and Gratitude

1. **Gratitude Practice**: Take a few minutes each day to reflect on what

you are grateful for. This can transform your mindset and improve your well-being.

2. **Acceptance of the Present**: Learn to accept circumstances as they are. Contentment comes from accepting the present without constantly desiring something different.

3. **Appreciating Small Things**: Find joy in the small daily things. A smile, a beautiful landscape, or a pleasant conversation can all be sources of gratitude.

Conclusion The jade Buddha teaches us that true contentment and gratitude are not linked to material things but to our ability to appreciate and fully live in the present. Cultivating gratitude and practicing acceptance helps us find lasting inner peace and profound satisfaction in our daily lives.

Part 4: Exploring and Embracing Zen Principles

Zen and Adaptability - How to Be Flexible and Adapt to Changes

Adaptability is a core principle in Zen philosophy, emphasizing the importance of being flexible and resilient in the face of life's inevitable changes. Just as water adapts to the shape of its container, we too can learn to adapt to our circumstances without losing our essence.

Lessons on Adaptability

1. **Acceptance of Change**: The first step towards adaptability is accepting that change is a natural part of life. Resisting change only creates stress and suffering. By accepting change, we open

ourselves to new opportunities and growth.

2. **Mental Flexibility**: Being mentally flexible means being open to new ideas and ways of doing things. This involves letting go of rigid thinking and embracing a more fluid approach to life's challenges. Meditation and mindfulness practices can help develop this flexibility.

3. **Resilience**: Adaptability requires resilience, the ability to bounce back from adversity. By cultivating resilience, we can maintain our balance and well-being even in difficult times.

Practices for Adaptability

1. **Meditation**: Regular meditation helps cultivate a calm and adaptable mind. It teaches us to observe our thoughts and emotions without attachment, allowing us to respond to change more effectively.

2. **Mindfulness**: Practicing mindfulness helps us stay present and grounded, making it easier to navigate change with clarity and composure.
3. **Positive Reframing**: Learn to reframe challenges as opportunities for growth. This shift in perspective can enhance your ability to adapt and thrive in new situations.

Embracing adaptability allows us to live more harmoniously with life's ebbs and flows, finding strength and serenity in the midst of change.

Zen and Patience - Cultivating Patience in Every Aspect of Life

Patience is a fundamental virtue in Zen, teaching us to live with calm and serenity by accepting the natural pace of life. Cultivating patience helps us handle stress, make thoughtful decisions, and build harmonious relationships.

Lessons on Patience

1. **Acceptance of the Present**: Patience involves accepting the present moment as it is, without wishing for immediate change. This acceptance helps us live with greater awareness and gratitude.
2. **Recognizing Our Limits**: Being patient means recognizing that some things take time. Accepting

our limits and understanding that not everything can be controlled or accelerated is essential for developing patience.

3. **Mindfulness Practice**: Mindfulness is closely linked to patience. Being present in the moment reduces impatience and helps us enjoy the small things in life.

Practices for Patience

1. **Daily Meditation**: Meditation is a powerful tool for developing patience. Spend a few minutes each day meditating, focusing on your breath, and letting go of hurried thoughts.
2. **Reflection**: Take time to reflect on situations that make you impatient. Ask yourself why you feel this way and how you can approach them more calmly and rationally.
3. **Gratitude**: Practicing gratitude for what you have in the present reduces impatience. Daily gratitude

exercises help shift your focus from what is lacking to what is abundant in your life.

Patience is not merely passive waiting but an active form of trust in the process of life. By cultivating patience, we can face life's challenges with calm and serenity, transforming difficulties into opportunities for growth.

Zen and Letting Go - The Importance of Letting Go of What We Cannot Control

In Zen philosophy, one of the deepest lessons is the art of letting go of what we cannot control. This practice frees us from unnecessary stress and anxiety, allowing us to live with greater serenity and awareness.

Lessons on Letting Go

1. **Acceptance**: The first lesson is to accept that some things are beyond our control. This includes external events, other people's behavior, and many life circumstances. Acceptance reduces stress and anxiety.

2. **Focus on the Present**: Letting go involves living in the present. We often worry about the future or dwell on the past, forgetting that the only moment we can truly live is now. Mindfulness helps us stay grounded in the present, appreciating each moment for what it is.
3. **Recognizing Our Limits**: Being aware of our limits is essential for letting go. Recognizing that we cannot control everything allows us to focus on what we can improve and influence.

Practices for Letting Go

1. **Meditation**: Meditation is a powerful practice for cultivating the ability to let go. During meditation, we can observe our thoughts without judgment and let them pass like clouds in the sky.
2. **Reflection**: Take time to reflect on situations that cause you stress.

Identify what you can control and what you need to let go of. Writing in a journal can be helpful for this process.

3. **Gratitude**: Practicing gratitude for what you have in the present helps you focus on positive aspects of life and reduces attention on what you cannot change.

Letting go of what we cannot control is essential for living a balanced and serene life. Through meditation, reflection, and gratitude, we can develop the ability to accept reality and focus on what we can influence. Zen philosophy teaches us that true freedom and serenity are found in letting go, allowing us to live with greater awareness and inner peace.

Zen and Gratitude - Practicing Daily Gratitude

Gratitude is a fundamental practice in Zen philosophy, helping us recognize and appreciate the small and large blessings of our daily lives. Practicing daily gratitude can transform our mindset, improve our well-being, and strengthen our relationships.

Lessons on Gratitude

1. **Recognizing the Good**: The first step in practicing gratitude is recognizing the good in our lives. This includes not only major achievements but also small daily joys like a warm meal, a friend's smile, or a sunny day.

2. **Appreciating the Present**: Gratitude helps us live in the present moment, appreciating what we have now. Often, we are so focused on our future goals or past regrets that we forget to enjoy the present.
3. **Cultivating Gratitude as a Habit**: Gratitude can be cultivated through daily practices. Keeping a gratitude journal, expressing sincere thanks to others, and meditating on gratitude are all effective ways to develop this habit.

Practices for Gratitude

1. **Gratitude Journal**: Write down three things you are grateful for each day. This practice shifts your focus to the positive aspects of your life and helps you recognize small daily blessings.
2. **Expressing Gratitude to Others**: Sincerely thank the people around you. Gratitude strengthens

relationships and increases your sense of connection and happiness. A simple "thank you" can have a significant impact.

3. **Gratitude Meditation**: Spend a few minutes each day meditating on gratitude. Focus your mind on what you are grateful for and let this feeling of appreciation fill your heart.

Gratitude is not just a response to positive events but a way of living that allows us to see the world with new eyes and appreciate every moment of our existence.

Zen and Connection - Connecting with Others and the Universe

Zen philosophy teaches the importance of feeling connected not only with the people around us but also with the entire universe. This deep connection helps us find a sense of belonging, purpose, and inner peace.

Lessons on Connection

1. **Empathy and Understanding**: Connection with others is based on empathy and understanding. Being empathetic means putting yourself in others' shoes, listening without judgment, and responding with kindness and compassion.

2. **Awareness of the Present Moment**: Being present in the moment is essential for connecting with others. Mindfulness helps us be more attentive and present in daily interactions, improving the quality of our relationships.
3. **Interconnection with the Universe**: Zen philosophy teaches that everything in the universe is interconnected. This awareness helps us see that our actions impact the world and encourages us to live more responsibly and respectfully towards the environment.

Practices for Connection

1. **Active Listening**: Spend time truly listening to others. Active listening involves paying attention without interrupting, showing genuine interest, and responding meaningfully.
2. **Meditation on Connection**: Spend a few minutes each day meditating

on connection. Visualize yourself as part of a larger whole, feeling your connection with others and the universe.

3. **Cultivating Meaningful Relationships**: Invest time and energy in relationships that matter to you. Show gratitude and appreciation for the people in your life and strive to build bonds based on trust and mutual respect.

4. **Respect for the Environment**: Recognize your connection with nature and the universe. Adopt sustainable behaviors, such as reducing waste, recycling, and protecting natural resources. This not only improves the environment but also strengthens your sense of connection with the world.

Conclusion Connecting with others and the universe is fundamental for living a balanced and satisfying life. Through empathy, present-moment awareness, and interconnection, we can cultivate meaningful relationships and live in harmony with the world. Zen philosophy guides us towards a deeper understanding of our place in the universe, helping us find peace and purpose in our daily existence.

Conclusion

Summary of Lessons Learned and Guide to Continue the Journey of Awareness and Inner Peace

We have journeyed together through the wisdom of Zen, exploring stories and principles that can transform our daily lives. Reflecting on what we have learned, it is clear that each lesson offers valuable tools for cultivating mindfulness and achieving inner peace. Here is a summary of the key lessons and some advice on how to continue this journey.

Summary of Lessons Learned

1. **Living in the Present Moment**: As we learned from Tenzin and the Master, mindfulness of the present moment is crucial for mental tranquility. Practicing mindfulness helps us stay grounded in the here and now, reducing stress and anxiety.
2. **Acceptance and Adaptability**: The story of the buffalo and the yoke teaches us that accepting what we cannot change and adapting to life's circumstances is essential for serenity. Emotional resilience allows us to face challenges with calm and determination.
3. **Compassion and Gratitude**: Cultivating compassion for ourselves and others, as demonstrated in Zen practice, enriches our relationships and emotional well-being. Daily gratitude helps us focus on the positive aspects of life, enhancing our overall happiness.

4. **Mental Flexibility**: Being open to new ideas and ways of doing things, as suggested in the lesson on adaptability, enables us to handle change with an open mind and a serene heart.
5. **Connection with the Universe**: Zen philosophy invites us to recognize our interconnection with everything around us. This sense of belonging helps us live in harmony with ourselves and the world.

Guide to Continue the Journey of Awareness and Inner Peace

1. **Daily Mindfulness Practice**: Dedicate a few minutes each day to meditation and mindfulness. This practice helps maintain calm and awareness in daily life.
2. **Reflection and Journaling**: Take time to reflect on the lessons learned and how you can apply them in your life. Keeping a journal

can be an excellent tool for tracking your progress and insights.

3. **Expression of Gratitude**: Every day, find at least three things you are grateful for. This simple exercise can transform your attitude and improve your well-being.

4. **Meaningful Relationships**: Invest time and energy in relationships that matter. Show empathy and understanding, and strive to build bonds based on trust and mutual respect.

5. **Connection with Nature**: Spend time outdoors, appreciating the beauty of nature. This helps you feel more connected to the universe and find inner peace.

Thank you for embarking on this journey of awareness and inner peace. Continue practicing these lessons and exploring Zen wisdom in your daily life, finding serenity and happiness along the way.

Made in the USA
Columbia, SC
25 September 2024

43031128R00043